I Was Never Broken

Volume 3

Moonsoulchild

I Was Never Broken: Volume 3

INTRO

Welcome back. Well, of course, only if it's your third time being here. If not, welcome. I don't want you to think you need to read these collections in order — but it may help understand my growth. If you're new here; this is my open journal. This is where I allow myself to be free and allow my vulnerability to shine in every way. I allow myself to be me, unapologetically.

I started the *first volume* at 16 and finished it at 25. I was going through a major life change. It became one of my favorite books because it captures honest feelings and of course, my voice. Something I lived through most of my life without.

The" **I Was Never Broken**" collection became a favorite worldwide. It's hit the best-seller charts on Amazon on multiple occasions. It received a lot of beautiful feedback and some not so much. I'm thankful for anyone taking the time to read my work regardless. The grammar might not be perfect and you may come across a mistake but the one thing I try to always bring is the ability to leave knowing we're all human and mistakes aren't something that defines us and the message is more powerful than the way it's spoken. I believe that's why we're here; to find ourselves in others, to find inspiration and healing. I am here to tell my story in the most imperfect way.

In this collection, I will include pieces I wrote back from when I was younger, which will include a time and date stamp or an acknowledgment that it was when I was (whatever age I was when I wrote it). The dates will not be in order. There are no sections. So, prepare for an **emotional roller coaster**. I also added little hearts on the end of the pages of my favorite pieces! I hope you enjoy this collection.

Most importantly,

> I hope you *hear* me.
> I hope you **feel** me.

NAMELESS

I developed this obsession with being known, to be set free. Being someone who stayed reserved and isolated, I was often imitated for my shyness and exploited for my silence. I never took a moment to love myself. I was often intimated, never liberated. I became a prisoner of my own reflections. I was far gone from who I once was. I broke myself down and resented who I've become. I had no mercy on my soul, there was no chance someone would waste their love on me if I couldn't even love my hardest when it came to me.

Someone **nameless** —
someone who feared being seen.

♥

December 17, 2022
11:07 PM

WANDERING HOUR

Sometimes I feel like I'm alone in this world, even in a crowded room I feel secluded. Everyone opening their mindsets but mine wasn't included. For the longest time, I feared my thoughts because they were never shared. I was a free mind scattered in a room full of simple minds. I felt caged and left silent. I thought my thoughts were waste because they were never filtered and always bottled. I thought my ability to connect with souls was my testament to being understood and out of this forsaken place, but it was only a hiatus. Being the charismatic, introverted, and free spirit I am, there were many bittersweet goodbyes and beautiful losses. I attracted all kinds of energy and sometimes the sentiment was lost and never found. The love was misplaced with hate. I was left unfulfilled, diluted, and left wondering if my essence would ever leave someone with anything more than a *paradox*.

♥

PIECES OF ME

Parts of me still live in the past because those parts of me died when those stories did. Parts of me live in fear because the unknown is terrifying; knowing forever isn't promised. Parts of me live within old lovers because they took a piece of me with them that I'll never receive back; a piece of me I no longer needed. Parts of me are still with old friends because we outgrew our story and the love still exists; just in a different form now. Parts of me still haunt me, the parts I couldn't love enough and I couldn't make peace with; they still urge me to pay more attention and give extra care. Parts of me still fear what could happen because nothing good ever came until I lived through the heartache.

I deserve someone who hugs me tighter on my darker days. Someone who doesn't judge or suffocate me when I need a moment to breathe. Someone patient and tender when holding my heart in their hands. I deserve someone who doesn't mix pain with love and creates an unhealthy environment to grow; someone who can flourish with me. I deserve someone who sees my value and doesn't downplay my potential; someone who showers me with praise and celebrates me, endlessly. I deserve someone who will love me, shamelessly. Someone who vows to stand the rain, the anxious outbursts, and sorrowful days without a source because the sun will always shine again. Someone who brings a force with them — a light. I deserve someone who doesn't just love me, someone who won't ever stop proving it. I deserve someone who brings me peace, someone who feels like home to me.

I vow to be this person,
to be this deserving because I will be this love for myself, first.

♥

My love language is creating a sanctuary you can come to whenever you feel the need to escape. I will be your safe place to fall. I will be your shield when you're at war. I will love you with all of my will. *I just hope you love me enough,* to not allow me to deprive myself of the same love I give you.

♥

I Was Never Broken: Volume 3

Please come whole if you plan to love me
I don't have what it takes,
to build a home
that's fitting for us two.
That's not love.

Please don't love me
if you don't possess the ability,
to love me to my core.
I don't have what it takes to teach you,
that's not fair to me.

Please don't stay in my life
just to lead me to a place of disappointment.
Don't allow me to sacrifice my worth
to save us,
when you know there's no rescuing us.

Please don't shatter my fragile heart
In a heartbeat
because you couldn't be bothered to be real.
Be honest with me.

Please don't love anyone
before you love yourself.
No one deserves to forget their worth
because the wrath of your selfish uses,
wait until you possess the power
to love what's within.
Don't do for love, what you cannot do.

♥

I Was Never Broken: Volume 3

You taught me —
infatuation is a phase
chemistry can burn out
connections can fade

You taught me —
love can be platonic
love can be demonic
love can be euphoric

You taught me —
everything is disposable
forever isn't forever
who we once were, isn't who we become

You taught me —
the most beautiful things can turn toxic.
Wasted time doesn't exist,
it's worth every moment spent.

You were a **teacher**
You were a teammate
You were a soulmate

If there's one thing I took from our connection, it's the
ability to always love my hardest even when I didn't
know if it would be reciprocated. *Life is most beautiful
when you expect the unexpected*, you can't be
disappointed.

♥

My *light*, you envied.
It threatened you
because you feared never knowing
what you'd become.
If you'd make it out of your darkness,
if you'd ever be enough.

I sympathize, I do
but the cost was too high.
I loved you,
but at the expense of sacrificing myself,
I'd rather pay my dues
than lose myself saving you.

I wasn't your healer, I was your friend
I wasn't your savior, I was your lover
I could only do and give so much.

    I hope my departure helped you see it
wasn't personal, it was needed for us both; to be
healthy versions of ourselves. I hope my absence
brought you the space to be brave enough to
discover yourself, love yourself, and unburden
yourself so you can make enough room for
someone to love you. I hope you finally do.

♥

NOVEMBER 11, 2022
2:09 PM

My last relationship taught me a lot about myself. It taught me to never settle for comfort, especially when it comes in many disguises. It was the cleanse I needed to create boundaries. It taught me not everything stays the same, even when love is involved, it can get messy and things evolve. It taught me baggage needs to be left behind and healed before stepping into love with someone else. I couldn't give someone the healthy love I needed to give myself, first. My last relationship taught me not everyone I love will be a connection that lasts a lifetime, sometimes it's a reflection of who I am in that moment. A *tribute* to old versions of myself I needed to deal with and heal. Versions I needed to stop missing so I could transcend into a healthier version of myself; one I could love, one I could stop hiding from.

♥

READ THIS BEFORE LOVING ME

If you're going to love me, know that it's not hard. I won't make you fight for my love, I will embrace you with complete openness; you will reside in my heart like the home you've craved. I will nurture you when you feel lovesick. I will be the friend you cry to, lean on, and always run to. I won't make you uncomfortable unless it's time to stand in your truth; my discomfort will only come in the form of helping your growth. I won't deceive you. I won't try to change you. I will always support you.

If you're going to love me, know that it may not always be easy. I am an intense lover, sometimes I may suffocate you. I'm an overthinker, extra TLC is recommended. I'm an empath, my emotions get the best of me; and get the worst of you, if you're not ready to embrace them. I don't think that makes me hard to love. I think it just means I was meant to be experienced differently. I think it means those who find me in this world were either meant to bring me love or bring themselves the experience they were missing within; both are a treasure.

❤

VOWS

I vow to embrace you tighter on your darker days but to hold you close to me every day after, too. I vow to pour into our cup as much as I pour into my own; to never drown or starve our love of the consistency it needs to keep growing. I vow to be your safe place to run to when you need protection; and your place of comfort when you need a quiet reflection. I vow to lift you on the days you find yourself dragging through. I vow to always remind you of your potential because you have shown me more than you can see. I vow to listen to you; I promise to hear you without making you feel like a hostage to your thoughts; because I know when they're dark, I can bring the light. I vow to never judge you and to always allow you to express yourself in the best way you choose. I vow to never deceive you, but instead, love you to my core, shamelessly because you are deserving of it. I vow to be your calm after every storm because our love will always stand the rain. I vow to always be the moon in your universe; to be your light as we both embody the essence of our union. I vow to love you and to always show you. I vow to never make you question it.

♥

BROKEN REFLECTIONS

I think there will always be a part of myself that requires extra TLC. I think I'll always look into the mirror and fear the revival of the versions of me that expired and faded with time. I think I'll always relive how brutal it was when I picked myself apart and let the skin I settled in, define me. I think when I see my reflection, I'll always visualize my flaws — I spent so much time trying to create a version of myself to diminish them. I think it's the voice in my head, the one that told me I wasn't good enough, the same one that always so desperately reaches out to chat. I think it's because for so long it defined me, it was my reasoning for everything. I think my obsession with being accepted had me chasing perfection and my not wanting to be perfect had me chasing this same vicious cycle of never being enough because I couldn't accept being imperfect is what fit me best. My heart was no match for those who couldn't love me — as I show up, flaws and all. *I had to give myself that love, first.*

♥

☾

MOON'S INTERLUDE

I don't miss old versions of who I was, those eras have vanished and never returned. Once I release them, I set them free to linger in the universe to undo this curse; to grace me with good karma. I vowed to never connect with those past versions. I made peace with the part of myself I couldn't love. *Good riddance* to the selfless, fear-driven, egoless version of me. **I'm ready to embrace** the emotionally gifted, bare, and mystery of who I'll morph into.

♥

Love isn't enough. Love is what ignites the connection, it's not the only thing that keeps it flowing. Being committed. Being loyal. Being present. Being open. Being honest. Having patience. Having an open mind. Having respect. Showing support. Showing your appreciation. Showing the love you express, not just in the form of words. *Love isn't enough* to hold things together that were meant to break. *Love isn't enough* to make someone love you the same. *Love isn't enough* to change someone, to save them from themselves. *Love isn't enough* to make someone stay after every mistake. I wish love was enough because heartbreak would have no place in my life.

The toughest thing I was taught was; *love was never enough*, but that didn't mean I wouldn't stop loving — it didn't mean turn cold. It just meant I had to accept every lesson of love and free the love I lost; to welcome the healthy love I made no place for. *It was unhealthy of me to believe love was a superhero.*

Teach people how to treat and love you by leading the way with the way you talk to yourself, treat yourself, and embrace yourself with the love you want returned. Allowing people to walk all over you without the boundaries placed and the ability to know what you deserve will only place you into a pattern of destructive love. Be the reflection of the love you want. The love you deserve will only come in the form of what you accept.

The love you find
will always be
a reflection of you.

I hope you keep your heart open even after you think it has failed you.

I hope you keep your heart open even if it bleeds onto the next one.

I hope you keep your heart open and realize your love isn't meant to be matched, it's to be experienced and not all experiences last in bliss, but that doesn't mean you close your heart off. You will do more damage freezing your heart.

I hope you keep your heart open because you deserve to keep loving even if it hurts sometimes.

I hope you keep your heart open because your love isn't meant to be found anywhere; that's what makes it special — it's one of a kind and someone out there may need it. I hope that's enough to always keep your heart open.

Endings are always painful. Sometimes they're bittersweet. Sometimes they hold a bigger blessing. Endings capture the essence of the connection in its entirety; you don't know what you truly have until it's checked out and you walk away. You see a clear vision when you're looking in from the outside. You find old red flags you packed away. You see someone for who they were the whole time. You see someone for who they grew to be as you slowly watched them drift away. Endings are new beginnings. Endings are hidden treasures; they build strength and character. Endings show you that not everything is meant for forever, sometimes it only hurts because we keep holding on when it's time to release what's meant to be set free. Sometimes we create more pain for ourselves trying to outlive a love that's never going to be.

I Was Never Broken: Volume 3

I hope you find the love that embraces you on the days you need it most, and every single day after, too.

I hope you find the love that doesn't make you an option because you are the only one.

I hope you find the love that **chooses** you.

I hope you find the love that brings out the fire in you, the love that moves mountains and diminishes fear.

I hope you find the love that doesn't doubt your heart, a love on the same frequency.

I hope you find the love that sees your vulnerability as a gift; a love that brings softness and a safe haven.

I hope you find the love that requires no sacrifice, that never makes you choose or give up anything that helps you grow and waters your soul.

I hope you find the love healthy for you, and this time you won't be afraid to embrace it.

SEPTEMBER 20, 2022
2:13 AM

FLEETING

I once thought seeking forgiveness from someone who destroyed me was necessary until I healed on my own without their permission. I tiptoed around the idea that my apologies could heal, so forgiving them for their brokenness would somehow complete us. A tough lesson I learned — it's not my responsibility to forgive someone who hurt me, to let them slide because they were lost, broken, and discovering. I don't need to carry that kind of resentment. I don't need it to forever burden me. I was once damaged, lost, and searching. I was the same wrecking ball that wrecked me. I'm not bitter towards anyone who brought me a great deal of pain. *I hope they find every piece of them and build a healthier version. I hope they can heal so they can find a love worthy. I hope they can finally love themselves too.* It's not about forgiveness, it's about letting go when it's time. Some things aren't meant to outlive their time.

♥

WRONG PERSON, RIGHT LESSON

I believe you loved me. I believe you loved me in the way you could without loving yourself. I believed you tried to express your love but it showed up flawed every time. I believe you wanted to give me the love I deserved, but you didn't know how to show up for yourself first. I believed you loved me but you couldn't make it healthy. I believed you supported me but you couldn't see my potential because you felt you didn't possess any. I believed you wanted to be good to me but you spent too much time on people who fill you with poison, you only kept yourself from goodness. I believed you could have been so much more but you let your past consume you and trap you until you became every bad thing that happened to you. I believed you wanted the best to come of us but you didn't believe it for yourself, so wrecking us was collateral damage. I believe you never wanted to intentionally hurt me. You were a good person—I saw who you were, at your core, but who you weren't kept you up at night. If only you could have loved yourself first, maybe we could have been, or maybe this is what we were destined to be. I loved to my core, and you tried to find love within.

We weren't meant to be romantic or platonic, nothing. We were meant to find the light we needed in each other, to see ourselves through our darkest hour. We were meant to learn from each other; and to align ourselves with the love that will embrace us, the love that we tried to find in each other but couldn't because we were teaching each other what we didn't deserve.

You will never know the ending of something when you first meet it, so give your all without giving yourself away. Love your hardest. Don't fear what could happen, it will take the beauty out of the story. Don't ruin the goodness of something focusing on the façade. Don't sabotage the bliss because you're afraid the story won't outlive the last one. You could pass up something remarkable living in the past tense; soak in the ambiance of what you have in the moment or you will forever wonder what it could have been when you had it.

People are allowed to walk away from you, they're entitled to their own journey, and if you're no longer a part of the story that's okay. You are allowed to be hurt by the outcome. You are allowed to feel emotionless. You are allowed to cage the anger in and feel betrayed. You are allowed to take the time you need to recover from the reckoning as long as you know they're also allowed to walk away and do what's best for them even if it costs you heartache. Sometimes things happen without a reasoning in place that could ever replace the pain or make up for it. Moving on is the only way to pass this time. You are allowed to feel how you feel, just like everyone else is too. We all feel things differently. We're all allowed to grieve differently. We're all allowed to do what's best for us, even if hurts, even if it's at the cost of someone else.

Sometimes people aren't ready to love you in the capacity you need them to. Sometimes they're not ready to love you at all. Sometimes they wish they could but they can't because they know they'll hurt you, believe them. Sometimes people need to work on themselves before stepping into love with anyone. Don't misinterpret this transparency as a reason to fight; sometimes it's no more than the truth being told. Sometimes you need to hear someone's intentions without letting yours be triggered. It's scary, to put your heart on the line, gamble it and lose, all because they raised the stakes. Sometimes it's not about you at all. Sometimes people aren't ready for something real. Sometimes they gave what they could until they couldn't. It doesn't mean you're not someone worth loving. Sometimes it's easy to get lost in something that feels good but instead of drowning you, they tried to save you the heartache.

Love yourself enough so when someone walks away, it doesn't feel like a death sentence, but instead, a rebirth. Take everything you learned and create something beautiful out of it because sometimes the things we wanted most are not always the best for us. Instead, they shape us and explain us in a way we haven't gotten to know ourselves. Understanding someone you once loved can be someone you love from afar is growth. Making peace with the end of an era, closing the book on forever. Accepting what's hurting you doesn't need to continue, set free what has outgrown you. *Love yourself enough* so you won't lose yourself trying to be enough for someone else.

HOPELESS HEART

If you ever get the chance to love, don't hold back; give it your all. Allow yourself to fall in love without the intention of being loved in return—it will be your greatest gift or your greatest lesson. You may feel if you put your all in and it is not reciprocated, you will lose everything, starting with your sanity. One thing is true, love will always live in you, you will always love even when you don't intend to—that makes it beautiful. I never believed love to be a choice because I never chose who I loved, it was a force that brought us together and the feeling was already there. I chose to be committed. I chose a relationship. I chose friendship. I chose to be loyal, to be honest. There is so much in life that can be chosen, but to love is not one of them because even when the ones we love walk away, we don't choose to not love them anymore, it takes time to grieve the loss and sometimes we're forever retracing the past trying to recreate the love we lost.

You deserve to be happy. You deserve so much more than what you're settling for. You deserve to start over whenever you need to regroup. You deserve to find comfort in spaces that don't make you settle, instead, create a space for you to be free. You deserve to feel loved because you're worthy of the goodness you possess, too. You deserve to receive the same treatment you put into the universe because your effort is proof enough. You deserve to be accepted into the spaces you seek refuge in because you are worthy of peace. You deserve to breathe. You deserve to take a moment to focus, to recreate a new path to align your journey. **You are deserving of every step you take to find your way back to yourself**. You deserve to seek love within, don't let anyone allow you to believe you don't deserve it.

The *biggest hearts*
always find,
the *coldest* love.

AT YOUR BEST

Even at your best, you may not be loved with the same love you give. Some people aren't ready to give that. Some people don't possess the capacity to love you with the love they are searching for within. You may come across someone who is at their best but it doesn't mean they're ready to love you. Sometimes they're simultaneously trying to be their best self without any interruptions.

Even at your best, you are love. You don't need anyone to validate you.

I no longer apologize for the parts of me that no one loved. I take extra care of those sides of me; I shower them with appreciation because they deserve to be treated with grace; they deserve to be held tenderly. I let too many people weaponize my flaws until I couldn't look at myself in the mirror without seeing their reflection of me. I no longer apologize for the parts of me that no one welcomed; they didn't make me less worthy, it wasn't ever my burden to carry.

5 WAYS TO HAVE A HEALTHY RELATIONSHIP WITH MYSELF:

1. *To treat myself* with grace and shower myself with patience. I deserve the same kindness I give.

2. *To listen* to my inner voice when it's uncomfortable. To never overlook, overthink, or overshare until I'm tired.

3. *Have self-talks* every time I need to be inspired. Speak positive affirmations when I'm struggling to see myself through the darkest moments.

4. *To never dismiss* my goals or desires — to indulge but to stand in my power. To always speak my truth and never silence my voice.

5. *To love myself* like I would love someone else — I deserve the same kind of effort.

SELF LOVE GARDEN

I planted seeds, I watered them
and watched them grow.
I poured every time I needed more
I nurtured until I felt I couldn't, anymore.
I trusted the timing.
I let it flow;
believing, loving, and sacrificing.
There's nothing I wouldn't do for love,
an *empowered* love, within.

♥

I forgive myself for selfishly wanting to be loved, I gave the best parts of myself to those who never took me seriously. I should have given that love to myself, first.

SELF-LOVE PARADOX

I hate public speaking,
but I love it.
My voice allows me to inspire.

I hate my acne,
but I love it.
It helped me look deeper,
to love what's within.

I hated my image,
but I love it.
It helped me understand self-care.

I hate overthinking,
but I love it.
It set me free from everything
that no longer served me.

♥

Self-love is
shedding the old layers
to make room for who you are becoming.
It is a homecoming
to the healthiest version of you.

FALL IN LOVE WITH YOURSELF

Fall in love with yourself. Fall in love with the intention to fall, but with the uncertainty of what is to come. Fall in love with chapters that are behind you, and the moments to come. Fall in love with the scars you hold, even if they can't be forgotten or forgiven. Fall in love with your flaws even if they can't be erased. Fall in love with your vulnerability, your wit, and your heart. Falling in love with your life is a form of self-care but loving the life you live is a form of self-love.

I don't think it's easy to embrace the goodness of
ourselves. Sometimes it is easier to adapt to
sadness because the consistency of it is
promised. Self-love is like hugging yourself
through the toughest moments, but the
embrace is not tight enough because we
always let our goodness slip through our
fingers—we forget our beauty once we
trade it to be loved and let down after let
down, we become destroyed and the
goodness we behold starts to crumble. We
lose every site of who we are and the
goodwill we possess. I don't think it's easy
to keep believing.

INNER CHILD VOWS

I vow to always love you at your best even when you are a mess. I vow to always hold you through your chaos and accountable for your madness. I vow to always listen to your inner critic, to always remind it you lived through it, you survived it. I won't allow it to control or consume you. I vow to never punish you for doing things out of love, even when it bruised you. I vow to always give you forgiveness and room to grow. I vow to always pour into you first before opening your heart to anyone. I vow to always love you even when it feels impossible. I vow to always love you more than the old version of you.

PROMISES

I promise to stop trying to fit into spaces I don't belong.

I promise to not over-compensate my love until it becomes loss.

I promise to never stay where I'm not loved.

I promise to remember my worth every time it's threatened, and all the time because **I AM ENOUGH**.

I promise to protect my heart at all costs.

I promise to seclude my soul from those who come to toy and destroy, to keep it sacred.

I promise to always sing the praise of my successes, to remind myself of every blessing.

I promise not to fall victim to old patterns, faces, or feelings.

I promise to only visit the past in reflections, dwelling is off-limits.

I promise to not allow temporary emotions to become permanent feelings.

I promise to always give myself the time, patience, and love I deserve.

SORROW OUTTAKES

Sadness was the soundtrack of my story for so long, I put my happiness on pause. I became a doormat to being who everyone else needed. Someone who was once so pure. I thrived in chaos; I made a home in people who ended up leaving me. I gained comfort from temporary emotions because I feared real love. I didn't fear how it would feel. I feared I wouldn't be worthy enough—so I would immediately ruin it. I was fixated on saving something I never experienced. There was no proof the love I was chasing was a sure thing.

UNNECESSARY SORROW

The love we shared seemed more like a business deal — *to heal each other*. We spent so much time filling each other's empty void, we didn't enjoy the company of each other. I was busy trying to be understood. I let you take your best shot with me. You were too busy trying to cope, to ever hold me the way I needed to be. We were never meant to become what we did. We could have saved ourselves the disappointment. We could have saved ourselves the lesson.

ROUTINE LOVE

I settled for struggle love because I thought the constant fight was worth it. I gave up some of my biggest dreams to be in the presence of someone I loved because I thought sacrifices needed to be made to survive it. I thought healing each other was the strongest commitment; until I was taken for granted and left stranded. *I settled for routine love* because I thought comfort meant security, but it came in the form of codependency. I settled for this stagnant relationship I couldn't afford to free myself of; the whirlpool of disaster I let it become because I thought love would be enough. I wish someone would have told me the love couldn't only be felt by me. I wouldn't have fought to be with someone who ended up a stranger.

I don't have it in me, anymore,
to keep giving myself to those
who only disappoint me.
Who only ghost me.
Who only pretend to love me.

My heart doesn't have the strength
to keep opening it to those —
Who have no intention of nurturing it.
Who won't protect it.
Who will only end up harming it.

You were lost
and wanted to be found.
I was searching and submissive.
We were synonymously rooted
in the same purpose — being *cherished*.
Except our definitions
were completely different.
Our lazy madness
of what we labeled *love*.

MY CONDOLENCES

I was ignored because of your bad day. A bad day that turned into months that festered into years without noticing I was suppressing my deepest emotions because I didn't want to be another burden. I wasn't the cause of your tension but you treated me like I was, I was the closest to you. We'd rise and dream next to each other. The silence became a pattern and I was left stranded in the dark. My love wasn't enough to hold you together. My ears weren't enough for you to unburden your soul. I was everything I could be for you until I could no longer be your refuge. The silence became a form of abuse. I was neglected and there was no longer a connection. Your routine of leaving me in the dark when you fought those demons that always come to haunt you. I was secluded because there wasn't anything more I could do so I decided to part ways. You needed to conquer this journey of

finding yourself alone. I was labeled
without a heart. I know I couldn't save you,
what you were going through was nothing I
could ever heal nor was it healthy for me to
try. If you never see me as the one who
loved you until our time ran out. I hope you
finally found happiness with yourself.
That's the bigger part of this story, not how
I let you go when you needed me, or how
you forgot to love me for me and not for
what I provided you. I needed to go, it was
time before I lost myself without the
remembrance of the good I behold.

I adored you more,
I valued myself less — *every time.*
I deserved to be longed
with the same affection I gave you
but you always left me
stranded,
No love found.

Wishing we could go back
to once we once were,
was a mistake.
What we had was misunderstood,
but I spent so much time
trying to make a wasteland beautiful.

I never said **I love you**
If I didn't mean it,
I won't lie—I'm not deceiving.
I can't say those words
If I didn't feel it.
So why did I always accept it,
from those who didn't mean it?

I was the reason for my heart's demise

If you push me away,
stay away.
Don't try to rekindle
what you gave away,
what we had,
what we **created**.
I'm tired.
I refuse to keep giving my heart
to those who treat it like a burden.
I'm giving my love
to those who are worthy.
I'm giving my time
to those who value me.

I once resorted
to being cold and locked away,
I forgot how soft my love was.

Shame on me
for always seeing the best in you,
especially when you didn't deserve it.
When you took my heart
and completely shattered it.

Shame on me
for thinking this time could be different.

I was consumed by your toxic ways,
forever spiraling into
your manipulative spell.
You'd push me away, **I'd stay.**
You knew your magic,
I was your greatest trick.

If you **push me away**
I promise you,
I won't be here when you return.
I don't have what it takes
to keep *breaking my soul*
just to feel your love.

NOVEMBER 6, 2022
2:06 AM

I needed to stop trying to make people see my perspective. I stopped trying to convince them to open their mind. It took me a while to see the compassion I was dealt wasn't always meant to be matched. The ego-driven souls weren't meant to be persuaded. It wasn't that I thought my perspective was the only direction—I just knew how much of a gift it was having a free mind, instead of being caged, like feeling lonely in a crowded room with no one who understood me.

DECEMBER 8, 2022
3:12 PM

I never thought of myself as someone who lit up a room, maybe because I was insecure, I couldn't see my power. People would tell me stories about myself but I couldn't believe it. Even though the one thing I always took pride in was my big heart, which cost me a lot of time and energy when it blinded me from any good because I lost more than I won. As time passed, I understood what they meant when they said I could bring a smile and a laugh without trying, that my aura brought a light they needed. I brought a safe place they felt secure in. Maybe it was trying that kept the fire going inside me. Maybe it was my kindness that kept me alive. Maybe it was the heart I have that always brought me closer to seeing what they always knew to be true.

I used to apologize for the days I couldn't smile, the days where laughter felt forced and I wanted to be in solitude. I thought it was wrong to seclude myself from the world but my thoughts were too provoking—I needed to sit with them, understand them, and set them free. I didn't like lashing out at anyone, making my burden another thing on their to-do list. I'd rather hide away until I feel whole again. It didn't mean I didn't love you; it was always about myself more than anything else. I found a sanctuary in myself, one I could always seek refuge in, one I felt comfortable yet powerful in. I won't be sorry for always choosing myself. I won't apologize for being selfish when it benefits me.

To not allow negativity to fill me with rage
and find its way to my most sacred place.
To allow myself to feel upset, angry, and
sad when it's fitting, but to never let it
overstay its welcome writing its way into
my life permanently. To not allow misery to
occupy my time and suck my energy until
I'm lifeless. To know everyone won't like
me, feel me, or ever wish to understand me.
That is something I'm learning.

To not allow everyone to occupy my heart space that doesn't deserve a place. A connection ignited but sometimes it's a spark and the flame burns out; sometimes it's for a moment and the moment fades. Sometimes what we once were isn't what we are forever. To love and hold the capacity to set them free when they walk away-- without resentment, without the fear of feeling like I'll never return to myself again. *That is something I'm learning*.

My love is too radiant
to be *felt* in the dark.

I vow to not search for love elsewhere until I have found love within. I vow to leave the baggage behind; to heal until it no longer hurts. I vow to keep my promises to myself. I vow to keep my love reserved for those who only create room for me to grow; not for those who absorb every single piece of goodness in me. I vow to no longer accept obligation as a form of acceptance. If you mistreat me, you will vanish from my sacred place. I vow to keep my energy reserved for those who bring the same frequency; to no longer allow everyone the same access to me. I vow to pay my unpaid debits; to make peace where I once created conflict. I vow to forgive myself for the times I thought I brought the best intentions but ended up being selfish. I vow to forgive everyone who brought me to the mercy of breaking because they were lost. I know loving me wasn't easy, too. I vow to always love the same; passionately and deeply; to never change my love language for anyone. I vow to never lose myself ever again, to be loved, accepted, or hoaxed by anyone.

I was judged by my flaws
before I could embrace them.
Which is why,
I spent half my life *trying to erase them*.

I VOW

To love me first. It was not about how I loved. I knew my heart was big and I was born to express my passion, it was more about giving that same affection to myself that I gave to everyone who never reciprocated a piece of that love.

I vow —
I would take care of my heart first.
I would take care of home,
I would love myself first.

LIGHT ME UP

When I think of you, I think of how
captivating you were. How your beauty
resembled the moon; how in every moment,
you shined bright, the tranquility in your
presence, you were a force. I remember how
the energy felt when you walked into a
room. I remember how deeply your stare
cut deep. I remember the imprint of your
smile. I remember it was the first time I felt
something honest. I'm torn because these
beautiful memories are lingering in my
heart and the loss of you takes up so much
space. Your departure haunts me. The only
thing that keeps me sane, is looking up and
being reminded that you're still near — you,
are the moon in every way, you light me up.
You are a force,
I'm forever missing you.

♥

BEAUTIFUL LOSSES

I will never heal from the loss of you, but I promise to never allow anyone to hold my sorrow. I will carry you with me but never allow it to burden someone else. I would never give myself to anyone if I can't promise them a healthy love. I promise to always cater to myself first.

MEMORY LANE

I am so afraid of letting you go — to allow you to transcend without it feeling like an emptiness within me. I am so afraid of losing you, that your memory will somehow fade as time moves. I fear what it would feel like because I struggle to not remember the pain but to remember you without feeling the weight of losing you. I am so afraid of one day not remembering the way your smile lit up the room or the way your aura shined through. I am so afraid of unremembering you. I am so scared of unloving you.

♥

COMMEMORATE

I said goodbyes to you a long time ago, but it still cuts deep. I still can't think of you without wishing we never parted. I still can't think of you without wishing we could have been something. I still can't think of you without feeling like I'm suffocating. The beautiful moments crowd my memory, but it's not long after they bring unwanted invitations to the heartache — the cycle continues.
Loving you is like Deja Vu, I know I won't be able to love another without remembering you.

♥

I once believed time healed all wounds. I always conflated healing with forgetting, somewhat suppressing. I thought in time it would feel less heavy, maybe escape my memory but now I believe time gives us the space to accept the losses, it doesn't give us true healing. It gives us the space to not allow the suffering to crowd us but that doesn't mean it still doesn't exist. I guess what they forget to say is when you dwell, it will come full circle. Because every time I remember you, the pain is excruciating, I seem to forget how to breathe.

Is that healing?

♥

I have found so much comfort in the moon since you transcended into the light of my universe. I search for you whenever you're out. Sometimes I look up and see you found me. I feel safe knowing you're protecting me. I feel my days are brighter knowing you're watching over me. Each day gets better but the grief still holds its place because I would do anything to see your face once more. I would do anything to look up at the moon with you once more, not look up and know it's you now. My mind replays the memories. The memories that fade with time. It's the pictures and videos that keep you alive, but it's my heart that works overtime to keep you surviving. I won't ever forget you. I don't wish to unremember you. I won't ever wish to unlove you. I only wish to never forget how your love impacted my life and your influence helped me choose the path I'm currently on. I only wish as time goes on, my love for you grows stronger even though every moment you're gone seems stagnant, there is so much force in your absence.

♥

I Was Never Broken: Volume 3

One of the most heartbreaking moments is someone being here; alive and healthy and gone the next without warning. After years of their absence, the pain still hurts like the moment they left. I no longer believe time heals all wounds, I think we just get better at carrying it.

It's been years of grieving and trying to heal from the loss. I accepted their absence but that doesn't mean it doesn't hurt like hell when I remember them. I cry my heart out when I see the memories. It's like losing a piece of your heart you won't ever get back or replace.

Sometimes the universe will bring you something you want just to show you its worth doesn't amount to yours. There's always a bigger picture. Sometimes the things you want aren't what's best for you, and *sometimes you deserve better*.

If you're unhappy in any aspect of your life, walk away from whatever it is that's making you so unfulfilled. Don't stay because you think it can be fixed. Sometimes things outgrow us before we realize.

Hold no resentment. **Hold no regrets**. *Hold no grudges*. Everything in life is written in a specific way, trust the timing. Sometimes there's no fix or rewriting—the best scenario is to keep the lessons, blessings, and every memory and walk away with grace. We outgrow people we love that we made a promise to, but time still passes and paths aren't always aligned. People outgrow you when you align with new versions of yourself. It's a part of life that's hard to grasp. The first instinct is to fight because love is involved, but even love isn't enough to hold together something that's outgrown you. The one thing that's overlooked and misunderstood is that we walk away without trying but every fiber of your being has tried, loved, and has told you it's time but you didn't listen. You can love everyone you love from afar. Take the heartache and make something beautiful from it. Don't drown and lose yourself within it. Outgrowing people and things we love is the scariest thing, but it's important.

Not everything lost needs to be found.
Not everything you lose is a loss.
Some situations are meant to *free* you.
Some experiences are meant to *teach* you.
Let them.

Not everyone who provided me
with a source of *comfort*
was good for my soul.

When you focus on yourself, everything that doesn't align with your boundaries will start to fade. Allow them to go and *transcend into something more beautiful*.

You're not obligated to keep opening the door for those who closed it on you and left you behind. You feel the need to keep circling back because they keep spinning back around. Unexpected returns are not déjà vu, they're reborn temptations to your fatal attraction.

- *Lessons of love*

Stop settling for someone who is there but feels out of touch.

Stop settling for someone who you found comfort in, but in the form of codependency.

Stop settling for someone who treats your vulnerability like a weakness when it's a victory; someone who dismisses your emotional intelligence, when they know it's because they can't amount to it nor do they wish to allow it.

Stop setting for someone who brought chemistry but lacked connection.

Stop settling for someone who brought a sense of lust until you no longer wanted to be touched.

Stop settling for someone because you love them; the love you once felt outgrew you before you knew. You don't need to stay in the same space anymore. Love isn't an excuse to fight for a connection that isn't healthy for you. Love isn't sacrificing everything that brings bliss to fill someone else up with that same happiness. Love isn't blind, it's tender. Love will never make you question if you're worthy. It will never make you believe you don't deserve it.

We fear letting go of something that once felt good because we fear we'll never feel something close; so we hold onto something that won't ever truly be ours. Love isn't an obligation; it's a testimony. Holding onto something that won't ever be yours will only keep you from falling into what's destined for you. It's promising to love again after being betrayed. It's promising to find happiness again, you need to be ready to set into the reality of sometimes love isn't enough to save what's outgrown you. It's promising to find someone deserving, once you become deserving of believing you are worthy. Stepping out of your past and writing a new chapter of your story. Highlighting the patterns you need to destroy. Cleansing yourself from the toxicity you let consume you and the traits you adapted to. Starting over can be terrifying if you keep replaying change in the form of never amounting to what once was. You need to be ready to embrace the beauty of what's to come, you are the only one who's holding you back.

I Was Never Broken: Volume 3

Love isn't easy to set free. Good memories invade your space. When you're someone who loves hard, the concept of letting go is terrifying even when it benefits you. I once kept hurting because someone I love was hurting too. I held on and took any damage from the outcome. I tried to help them find the light. I tried to unlock the hidden gem I saw in them, except it wasn't my doing so I got hurt in the process of trying to heal them. Love wasn't enough to save someone from themselves, especially when they don't believe they're worthy. I've been wrecked by some who came to destroy. I've been hurt by some who used my love as a weapon, and some who used my love as a pawn to be good enough for someone else. They took my heart to a place that feel good until they abused it. I could make excuses — they didn't have the heart to love me because they weren't aware of their worth, but I won't. I didn't deserve to be stripped of my worth at the cost of theirs. I didn't deserve to go through hell just to be left broken. It wasn't their job to show me my worth or to make me feel like I was enough, but when you take my heart and promise to keep it safe just to leave it broken. My heart is built differently. I'll walk away with grace but don't ever expect me to have remorse for someone who couldn't give me what they knew they couldn't but still made me believe they could.

Too many times we see people hurting and we feel we can be their savior. We feel if they fall we'll be able to catch them every time. We know what we're capable of when it comes to our hearts and the lengths we go to for someone we love. That's why when we put out all in and it's not enough we feel the pain cut deeply. We don't see it as overstepping, we see it as over-loving. We don't see it as overcompensating our heart, to work in overdrive, we see it as being there no matter the cost or circumstance. There's nothing we won't do for love. We don't see it could also be our fault because we put ourselves on the battleground without a shield or armor. Too many times people don't ask to be saved, but we extend our superpowers for as long as we can until we're the ones in need of saving.

♥

I can't save anyone from their trauma.
I can't make anyone change.
These have been the hardest lessons of my
life—letting loved ones go because they're
toxic to their being. I couldn't stick around
and watch them destroy themselves.

I knew it was time to let someone go when I gave all of me to the point there was no more to give. When they didn't question my absence. All the chasing trying to prove my loyalty, when they decided not to meet me halfway.

People can love you
even if they don't love themselves. Love is a
feeling. It doesn't mean it will be healthy or
the way you deserve. They will love you the
best way they know, while you need to
choose if the capacity of love they provide is
enough for you.

OCTOBER 9, 2022
11:48 AM

Walking away from everything that no longer serves you. I never said it was easy, but for me, it was needed to grow. Walking away from everything that no longer served me gave me a life filled with so much purpose. Five years ago, I wouldn't be where I am today if I didn't choose the path I'm on right now. The littlest things can change in the matter of one decision. You don't need to soak in your miserable life when you can choose to move on at any time. You don't need to be unhappy just because you don't believe there's anything else out there for you so you decide to settle. Some people will read this and believe this is a fantasy or that you should, "suck it up and live your life and deal with your problems", but there's a huge difference between dealing with problems and living a life that's outgrown you. Staying in a toxic relationship will only destroy you. Staying in friendships that you outgrew and on a different path can turn toxic if you hold high expectations of the past. Staying in anything that's a cycle of nothing good will leave you unhappy, unbalanced, drowning in regrets, and wondering what could have been if you chose differently. Don't be afraid to move on when your intuition has spoken. I was afraid to walk away from everything I once knew, people I loved, and a life I settled for. I couldn't imagine hurting anyone even though they hurt me. I couldn't imagine walking away when comfort was in place, but for the first time in my life, I took a chance and chose to be uncomfortable to grow. I stepped outside of my comfort zone and chose to walk away from everything I once knew to embrace a life I had no control over. Here I am, five years later; happy, in love, inspired, and fulfilled. I couldn't imagine staying with someone who didn't believe in my dream. I couldn't imagine staying on a path that lead me nowhere. I couldn't imagine living in a cycle of never feeling good enough and always living in fear of the unknown. I broke out of my shell and grew into this beautiful human with a beautiful soul, who found a beautiful life. I'm so blessed.

OCTOBER 6, 2022
1:04 PM

When it comes to connections, we share different ones with different people in our lives, no one connection is the same. Some connections end badly so it hurts to remember. Some connections damaged you and the repair is still taking a toll on you. Sometimes the healing hurts more than the illusion you set yourself to believe. Sometimes people outgrow each other, sometimes it's not deeper than that. Someone once told me that the term "outgrowing" is a term used out of context — that the word "narcissist" is the better term because someone always hurts someone and that's why the connection ends. I don't see the truth in that. I've loved people who I loved and had no ill intentions towards moving on, we just weren't meant to keep our story going. It takes a great deal of courage to separate yourself from the idea that pain needs to live in every disconnection. The pain comes from the thought of moving on because you love someone and the mind and heart fight over what you should feel. Sometimes things happen and you convince yourself it was more searching for answers to a question that doesn't have more to explain other than it's time to move on.

Outgrowing isn't easy, but sometimes it happens before you realize it without bad intent. Outgrowing is peaceful once you realize you don't need to grieve this person in the worst way but can love them and still let them go. Sometimes you can keep them in your life, but the connection is just different. We grow and go through many changes. No one stays the same forever. The love you once shared with someone years ago can run its course if you're on a new path to finding yourself. Keeping the mindset that you will stay the same, love the same, and keep the same people in your life forever brings the hardest lesson when it comes to detaching from them, the promises you once made, and the idea of what once was. If you truly believe you can't outgrow a lover, a friend, a job, or anything in life, you will always stunt your growth holding hostage things that no longer serve you. It's time to free yourself.

DECEMBER 31, 2022
3:33 PM

Some of my biggest tragedies are behind me, but that doesn't mean they'll be forgotten, it doesn't mean there won't be more. My trauma is a layer within me that taught me so much about loving and letting go. My trauma taught me how vital it is to heal just enough so I don't settle in sorrow and make comfort a permanent home. I've cried enough tears to last a lifetime. I've picked up pieces and tried to repair connections that were never meant to be replaced. I overstayed my welcome in lives I had no business taking up space in. I over-loved, over-compensated, and over-valued time, energy, and expectations. I spent a lot of time lost, disappointed, and overwhelmed by the lack of passion I had most of my life. I don't live in that realm any longer. These past four years have been a blessing. I sing a different tune now, one of authenticity, vulnerability, and soulful bliss. I take the challenges of life and create something beautiful because life is too short to soak in the darkness. It's too short to live chasing things I won't get back. I grieve differently, I take the loss and soak in it just enough to feel it, to find the beauty in the wrenching pain because it's the only way through, the only way to heal the wound. I find everything in life so incredibly inspiring. I've dreamt of the life I'm currently living. I have a passion flowing through my heart and soul like never before. I have met souls who align with my spirit. I have accepted blessings that are a match for me. I live for the present and not a day in the past. I live for the gift of being my authentic self. I'm in tune with my emotions. I'm in tune with what feeds my spirit. I won't allow misplaced hate bring me to a place of anger. I won't allow misdirected anger bring me to a place of rage. I will keep calm. I will never forget I was once that misunderstood, broken, and lost individual. I will always lead with empathy, but I will still block what doesn't align with me. I pray for everyone soul searching. I pray everyone finds a healthy love, especially within. I won't allow fear to fester and be my narrator, I will always conquer. I will always love, grow, and be more resilient. Over the years I thought living was about surviving but it's about feeling alive. It's about being happy. It's about peace. I was living wrong for so long but at this very moment in time—I'm happy, I'm healthy, and I'm at peace. I won't ever take this life for granted. It's the only one I got.

Chaos comes in the form of comfort when you
find yourself attaching to things that need
your attention. Unhealed souls that need
saving. Broken hearts that need repairing.
Continued patterns of lust that are confused
with love. Chaos seems enchanting because
of the constant upkeep to keep the story
going. The chaos we indulge in becomes a
bad habit we fall victim to, more times than
we plan to. Once we believe chaos is the
story we've embarked on and embedded
into our journey, it's hard to imagine
calmness. Once you accept chaos as
something keeping you from everything
written for you, you will see the
misconception that has been blocking your
direction. Chaos will no longer be your best
option, it will be the friend you let go of, the
one that was toxic waste to your being. *Free
yourself from everything fleeting*.

♥

Good things don't last forever. Sometimes they outlive their time and you find the next best thing. Don't miss the beauty of what's awaiting you, chasing the climax of a chapter that no longer holds purpose.

On this battlefield, one I created for myself trying to make you feel me. I stand here without any armor or shield to protect me. I took my best shot and it misfired. I should have spent more time learning how to be deserving instead of teaching you to love me. I should have spent more time protecting myself instead of waiting for you to validate me. I should have listened to your ultimatums and recognized your red flags instead of trying to fight for a bond that was conditional, unfair, and misconstrued. I should have guarded my heart instead of giving you a dozen second chances to ruin me.

♥

You will always be enough for the right person. The person who doesn't allow you to settle, but encourages you to realize your potential. The person who stands by and watches you bloom — who pours into your cup when you're running low, to fuel the self-love in you. You will always be enough for the person who understands your heartache, acknowledges your scars, and sympathizes with your losses. A person who doesn't hinder your recovery or make you feel ashamed of your past. The person who is inspired by your dreams and ambitions — who doesn't silence your fears, but instead, allows them to have enough room to grow into triumphs. The person who creates a space for you to be your authentic self without trying to dim down your emotions, ego, or vision. The person who will also check you if you need realignment. You will always be enough for the person who chooses you. The person who is the right amount of love, inspiration, and refuge you need. You will always be enough for the right person, once you believe you are deserving of it.

♥

After all the heartache of chasing what wasn't meant to be yours, the journey back to yourself will be long, daunting, and chaotic; but it will always be worth the outcome.

HEARTBREAK 101

A broken heart won't be completely mended. It can't be fixed or replaced. You will remember every heartbreak. You will live with the loss. A healed heart will only create a shield for the suffering. A healed heart will only make you stronger in understanding loss. So, don't be so hard on yourself. It's okay to not be okay. It's okay to take as much time as you need to recover from what you're hurting from. It's okay to soak in the feeling a little longer than some might recommend. There's no time stamp on healing, there's no right or wrong route to take. You will heal on your own time. One thing that doesn't change is a damaged heart will always be broken because the people you love and the moments you lived will never be forgotten, you just meet a new version of yourself after each heartbreak.

DEPTHS OF YOU

I was always intrigued to dive deeper into someone's mind. I wanted to know the layers of themselves they tried to hide. The layers of them only they could find. I wanted to know what thoughts kept them up at night. I wanted to pick their mind and learn the parts of them they try to cover up and erase. I wanted to learn their love languages so I could speak to them in the same language. I wanted to help them achieve their definition of happiness by standing by them while they stand in their truth. I wanted to unleash the skeletons in their closet to understand the scars they hold. I wanted to seek their darkness so I knew how to hold them; so I knew how to be their peace. I was always interested in every connection that had my heart invested. To me, it was how I loved and how I showed up, it was never about it being reciprocated, but it was somethin' special when it was returned.

♥

Sometimes it comes down to choosing yourself or being chosen by someone else. You will always chase love when you're waiting to be validated by someone who can't hold you in the ways you need to embrace yourself. You will always align with the wrong person when you seek to be chosen instead of loved.

Choosing yourself is freeing, waiting to be chosen by someone else is fleeting. You will always chase the feeling and be left unfulfilled. The most beautiful things transpire once you find your way back to yourself. When you decide to choose, find a home in your solitude and fall in love with your aloneness. When you choose to lift yourself and hold yourself through your darkness. When you choose to stand in your truth instead of running from it. When you choose to dedicate every moment becoming a better self instead of finding someone to fit perfectly with you. When you choose yourself, you're choosing the direction your life's about to take. You're choosing to align yourself with everything set to cross your path without knowing what it could cost you, but always knowing the outcome will pay off. Always choose yourself.

DEAR YOU

Please, be *vulnerable*. Wear your heart on your sleeve. Don't allow anyone to diminish your worth or dim your potential. Being "too emotional" isn't a threat, it's a force not everyone can reckon with. It means you hold the capacity to bring a great deal of love and a great deal of pain, but with your soft heart, your intentions are pure. You're connected, aligned, and in tune. You can feel the energy shift in a crowded room. Your intuition speaks — you listen. You don't ignore the cycles of your emotions, even sadness has its right to occupy you, but never allow it to crowd you. You thrive when you're emotionally connected. You create connections through emotional intelligence, you're a sucker for those who share the same values — those who embrace your naked soul because they value you.

It's always a beautiful thing
when we finally discover
the softest love
after the coldest.

Healthy love
isn't sacrificing anything,
but your old idea of love.

LOVE AFFAIR

I want you to know, you are more than just another love I've come to know. You are the love that stops time and made me realize every bond before this was just an idea of love I created because of the tenderness you shower me with, which I never witnessed up close. I want you to know the space you give me when I need it, it's appreciated. I cherish your closeness and how you allow me to breathe. I treasure how communication is always first—no secrets are ever kept; we've been revealing our deepest darkness since we met. Our love developed quickly but it's grown so much over time, it ages so beautifully.

♥

You're the balance my heart needs.
My heart has felt
so safe, comfortable, and alive
ever since you opened it.

SURE THING

Falling in love with you was easy, there was nothing complex about the way you were ready to embrace me. I fell in love with the way you met me halfway; no pieces to pick up, no ulterior motives. You were ready to love me with your heart open and your soul naked. You walked into my life when I was discovering who I want to become. I was setting boundaries. I was breaking bridges. I was building foundations. I was seeking forgiveness. I was choosing me. I was searching for peace, and I found you, someone who brought the softest touch to my heart and ignited my soul. I knew at that moment—no storm could destroy, no darkness could diminish and our love was a sure thing.

♥

5 WAYS TO GROW WITH SOMEONE

1. **Be an open book**. Don't be afraid to ask questions. Don't tense up when asked tough questions. Your past is behind you, don't be ashamed to have that conversation. Being open and honest can either bring you closer or apart. Someone who accepts you; flaws, scars, and all; that's honest. Some people can't handle honesty because it's not their policy, but that's only setting you free, you can't go wrong.

2. **Support them**. Support each other. Show up when it's time. Show the love instead of always speaking it; shower them so they can feel it. Be genuine and be present—it's one of the most meaningful things; feeling love and believing it.

3. **Express your feelings**. Speak your desires. Uncover your heart. Vulnerability is your greatest gift; using it wrong will only hurt you and everyone else.

4. **Don't expect** them to be a mind reader; listen and not just respond, hear them out, and console them. Be the one they run to, the one they come home to after a long day. Just let them vent to you, sometimes it's just knowing you're there that makes them feel heard.

5. **Be the safe place** they find their peace. The energy you possess goes a long way.

SEPTEMBER 23, 2018
10:29 P.M.

I still dream of you. I still gaze at you and wonder how I was matched with someone that deserves the love I give. I wasn't fully prepared to take on our love. I don't think I was fully equipped to embrace our love so freely; but I promise you, once I did, I never thought of letting it go. Spending years of my life dreaming of the perfect love, to spending years of my life with the wrong ones; I was led to you. I wish time didn't need to teach me a lesson. I wish it didn't cost me every disappointment, every minute wasted — but those wrong ones shaped me and gave me the courage to keep loving. I refused to believe love was pain. I refused to believe the love people tried to poison me with.

People would ask me "how did you get so lucky" but to me, it's not luck. It's giving your heart, all in, every time. It's never giving up when all you wanted was

to give in. It's never letting your pain
change you or the way you love. It's never
allowing the illusions people made love be,
a reality to you. It's not luck; it's patience.
It's getting hurt repeatedly, trying to make
everyone love you because you thought it
was a cure for your emptiness. It's watching
the ones you thought loved you, turn into
someone you thought you knew.
So, luck isn't the word I'd use. I would say
I'm blessed. Blessed to have found the love I
prayed for after many sleepless nights.
Blessed to have found someone I can be
fearless with; someone who loves me the
way my soul needs.

It wasn't hard to love you, you made it easy.
Every day with you feels like the greatest
day of my life. I don't ever wish to see a day
without you.

Your love is my muse. When we met your heart felt like an open invitation to our forever. I knew there wasn't anything else destined for me. It started and ended with you.

The most beautiful kind of love is the love that holds no limits and keeps on giving. There's so much beauty in love that's not forced, and the connection was created on its own. Falling in love with someone for who they are is something life-changing. You fall in love with the person deeper than their exterior; you fall in love with the depths of their soul.

Maybe right now your journey isn't about finding love; maybe it's about discovering yourself in every aspect before you step into the chapter of loving anyone or letting them love you. Maybe right now it's time to focus on what you have and not what you desire, but to plant the seeds for what you want and water it until it grows; and if it doesn't, don't give up, try a different direction. We focus on what we want and never focus on where our life is at this current moment. We forget this is exactly where we need to be. We forget there's so much to life because we latch onto what we don't have. We tend to live in the past and the future but never in the present moment. We take for granted the greatest moments because they're not what we expected, without realizing expectations kill every thing. Maybe your journey isn't where you want to be, but it's where you need to be, so embrace the ride.

THINGS I'LL NEVER FORGET

1. *Giving* myself away to people without having a return date to myself.

2. *Putting* my heart on display only to have it cost me.

3. *Letting* go of people I never thought I'd outgrow or unlove.

4. *Grieving* a loss I couldn't prepare for, one I shouldn't need to live through.

5. *Secluding* myself from everything I loved, to be someone else's safe place.

6. *Never* speaking up for myself or standing my ground; letting my voice be at the mercy of everyone.

7. *Being* loved wholeheartedly to my core, by those who never failed but to learn me, see me, and show up for me. Those who loved me because of me, not for their need.

8. *Always* believing my heart was treasure and my soul was gold.

Being honest without caring what it would cost me. *Addicted to realism*. Addicted to only attracting what's meant for me.

Happiness was never about fitting in and being validated.

Happiness was never about what job you chose or what your future held.

Happiness was never about how many friends you ended up with or how much you were accepted.

Happiness was never about looking your best and striving to be perfect.

Happiness was never about finding the right person to love and hoping they would love you back.

Happiness is doing what you love to do without having any expectations.

Happiness is about embracing what you have and not waiting for what you want.

Happiness is indulging in your desires without having shame.

Happiness is in everything we create; it's the peace we make for ourselves in everything we choose.

Don't search
for the old versions of yourself,
they don't exist anymore.
It's time to face your growth.

I Was Never Broken: Volume 3

Many won't know how to love you and it's not your job to teach them.

Many will treat you like you're hard to love because they can't love themselves and it's not your fault.

Many will destroy all the good left in you, or try because they can't seem to find the good in themselves. Their insecurities aren't your responsibility to soothe.

Many will mistreat you and blame you for their mistake because they know they don't deserve you. It's not up to you to save them, save yourself instead.

Many will love you, but not in the way you deserve, it's up to you to determine how far you'll let it go.

Someone who takes the time to listen to you, get to know you and understand the depths of your heart and soul won't ever need help to love you, it will be easy to. You will never be good enough for someone who isn't ready to love you. There's no saving that can make you see how you wish they could. Wish them well but know there's someone out there that won't make you feel hard to love because you are not.

.

I don't match energy. I always give the most even when it's not deserved. I take pride in sharing my heart with the world, even if it will hurt me more than benefit me. Someone may have needed the experience more than me. I know we're all searching for something. I know we're all longing to be loved.

I was made to believe my emotional depth
was unstable, so I turned cold and
abandoned my own heart for the sake of
someone else's acceptance.

I won't ever apologize for the way I love.

Accept that your emotions change like the seasons and take the opportunity to release and heal. Everything that leaves your life creates space for something better to bloom. Keep repeating that until you believe it, until you feel it.

It was rare when I let someone in because of the way my heart beats, no one could match the rhythm; no one could understand the lengths I'd go to for someone I cared for. I was always loved with conditions, ones I didn't set.

No one ever took the time to learn me.

We let go of people because we outgrow them before we realize, sometimes we screw up and sometimes they hurt us. Sometimes we have no choice but to move on without an apology, without the choice to redeem the relationship; but also the choice to redeem ourselves. We let go of people we wanted to keep around us for lifetimes, but their story no longer aligns with ours. We let go of people who damaged us for the next one and we have no choice but to pick up the pieces and recreate ourselves again, from the beginning, without the love we yearned for or the love within. We lose every trace of figuring out how to love again, smile, and live without feeling caged. We let go of people we love and sometimes it's harder than we realize when we live in their absence until we can't love another without their permission until we accept we are far more worthy than the validation and love we searched for within them. We let go of people we love, which was out of our control, and it will hurt until it no longer feels heavy, but the scar will always be there and we will always outlive the pain of before.

OPEN HEART, CLOSED SOUL

My soul is my sacred place, not many have made their way to reside there. My heart was the space everyone occupied. Open heart but my soul was closed off. It was easy to love, but it was harder to let myself be loved. I couldn't let everyone in and know the deepest part of me, to my core, that would be an open invitation to break me. When someone stepped into my soul, they either broke me or taught me a valuable lesson of myself.

I'm someone who protects my aura at all costs. I feel heavy about my character; I know what I'm worth and I won't let it be threatened. I'm someone who gives my last to help another; my heart is too big to allow my love to go to waste. I'm someone who doesn't limit my love, I never was too cautious with who I allowed in my sacred space; I knew even the battered souls possessed goodness too. I'm someone who took a chance and didn't let it down when it failed me, I was never the type to give up — I'm someone who gave all of me without permission to receive the same in return. I'm someone who lost and found myself again and through the darkest moments, I created light to see myself through. I'm someone who never let this cold world break through, every storm never kept me from shining. I'm someone worth loving. I'm someone worth remembering.

♥

SURVIVING MY TWENTIES

My twenties were an experience, one I will
cherish no matter the circumstances of the past. I
loved and lost some of the greatest souls, and
some ended up a lesson of what love wasn't. I
ghosted and walked away from people without
leaving a trace of understanding but through the
process, I learned transparency and the ability to
communicate with honest reflection. I once
feared hurting the ones I loved because I feared
being hurt myself, my heart extended that far
and my empath poured over every time. I made
mistakes out of the best intentions. I never led
with a bad plan, sometimes I just allowed my
anger to get the best of me. I think it's very
human, but I know I need to be better. My
twenties were all about discovering me—the
highs and the lows. Putting myself together and
seeing what fuels me ignites me, and keeps me
loving. I went through many phases; I had my
gloomy days that flowed into depression, and
anxious nerves that kept me from my desires. I
found comfort in the form of codependency.
Being a shy soul my whole life I know I needed
someone extroverted to bring the liveness out of

me. I couldn't contain myself and expected to grow. I met a lot of discomfort but it helped me change my direction and get myself on the right path. My twenties were about breaking and being reborn. My twenties were about communicating and building a foundation. My twenties were about creating the boundaries of setting the tone of the life I wanted. My twenties were about understanding, forgiveness, and so much self-love. People always said "live your best life in your twenties" so I tried, but with that notion, I felt depleted because I lost myself in the sorrow of every loss—I felt like a failure. People act like your twenties are your best era, but every moment you have alive is the greatest. I've grown wiser. I've grown more resilient. I can say I love myself—I love the life I've lived and continue to build.

Don't let anyone tell you that your best life is in your twenties. It's your era of learning, understanding, and growing. There's so much that continues to happen that adds to your story, a story that never ends as long as you're here to keep writing it. Don't fear the unknown, embrace it. The best happens every moment you continue to try.

DEAR SELF

You are going to make mistakes, lots of them. You don't need to be perfect to be successful. You will make it as long as you're dedicated and motivated, passionate too. You will fall more times than you'll stand but you will achieve no matter the circumstances. If you put in the work you will always find a way. You are going to feel uncomfortable and lost at times, but you will always find your way back and your way through.

Our time expired years ago. Our connection still lingers in my heart. My love for you still exists. That's why it will never not hurt to be without you. Even though we rekindled, forgiven, and grew. We're far from what we once knew. We're strangers.

I miss you,
I miss my best friend

I outgrew the old,
to **grow** into the new.
Every lost connection
was a new beginning,
to a different version of me.

My *unhealed self* would indulge in chaos
because it made me feel something of
purpose. I got trapped in the habit, I kept
the cycle going. I attracted everything
broken.

My **healed self** still fights the urge to fall
back into patterns of being the one who
bleeds on everyone else—just to heal them.
I don't search for chaos, sometimes it finds
me. I stopped giving away my power to
what breaks me down. I started attracting
less of what hurt me.

In my past every time I thought I was in love, I came to the realization, it wasn't love if I had to chase for it. It wasn't love if I had to prove my worth. I stepped away from wanting to find love within people who didn't have love to give me, that's when love discovered me.

DECEMBER 16, 2022
2:07 PM

The power of believing is everything. All those negative thoughts hindering your mind that you allow to manifest in your everyday life will have you far from what you want deep down. Be careful how you talk and treat yourself. Be careful what you put into the universe—your message might end up translated differently if you give the power to your negative thoughts.

Nothing good ever came my way when I was sunken into darkness and suffering. I wanted so badly to be loved and understood, but I allowed my sadness to control the narrative. Instead of speaking to myself with grace, I replayed the same old song. I sounded like a broken record when it came to all the betrayals and misfortunes. I did nothing to create a different story. it wasn't until I started to believe I deserved better, better started forming. It wasn't until

I spoke to myself with kindness… I was treated with grace. It took a while to believe good things would happen to me because of the constant letdown, but my desire to want more and attract better was far more powerful than drowning in sorrow. I had to see *I was deserving of everything I was once accepting*. To want better **I needed to be better**. To get everything I deserved I needed to stop believing I wasn't worthy of anything good. It wasn't my fault how some treated me but it was my responsibility to not think everyone would treat me the same because if I allowed that feeling to thrive, I wouldn't ever be worthy.

I'm mature enough to forgive people in this lifetime for the time they treated me less because their insecurities shined brighter. I'm mature enough to see the difference between hate and someone who's lost. I was once foreign to myself, so if you treated me wrong under the circumstances, I forgive you. I pray you are at a place in your life where you're happy and at peace. If you're still soul-searching, I pray you're closer to identifying. I'm mature enough to know sometimes we love people who were only meant to be a moment. I'm mature enough to not hold regret towards the same people who brought more pain than love. I'm always praying for love, happiness, and peace for everyone I loved and lost. Our paths are no longer meant to align. Our souls found a deeper connection within. Where we were headed didn't match, it made sense until it no longer did. The love still holds weight on my heart—as you will always be remembered but I'm mature enough to know the difference between loving and letting go, and how sometimes you feel both at the same time. I'm mature enough to admit I held some toxic traits too, and how I let myself be consumed. I'm mature enough to admit I wasn't perfect, I brought pain too. I'm mature enough to admit to everything I brought to the connection, I only wish to receive the same closure.

IN CASE YOU FORGOT

Be gentle with your heart, it's fragile. After all the pain, handle yourself with care. You didn't escape everything that once came to destroy you, just to return to another relentless goodbye.

I feared comfort
the moment I realized,
I settled because it was familiar
not because it made me happy.

Being an introvert didn't mean I wanted to be lonely. I just wanted someone to understand me enough to make me feel safe. Being an introvert just meant I was a little harder to uncover. I am a treasure worth discovering.

I lost myself within you.
I lost every part of who I wanted to be,
when I became a part of you.

Don't let anyone tell you how to wear your emotions. Wear your heart on your sleeve. Express your vulnerability. You're capable of feeling everything so deeply, it's a blessing and a curse—but it's always a gift. Cry when you need a release. Allow yourself to soak in the emotion you're currently feeling; but don't let it consume you. It will pass, just like a bad day, it's a phase unless you keep dressing yourself the same. Let it flow, let it go.

EFFLORESCENT

You can't plant seeds and expect them to grow without nurturing them. Watering them from time to time isn't going to help them blossom. Giving half attention and expecting full effort will dehydrate you. It's not going to work. You can't give part-time love and assume everything will find its way. Take care, give tender love, and patiently wait. You can't rush timing; the most precious things take time.

I once thought *love*
was the cure for loneliness,
until I fell in love with someone
who made me feel lonely.

Allow them to stand in their truth,
that kind of love
stands the test of time.

I think everyone deserves to find that one
person who makes all the difference.
I think everyone *deserves a healthy love*.

The darkest moments hold the most light. Don't ever surrender, there's always time to rewrite. Feel free to escape when you need space. Never punish yourself for feeling; your vulnerability is the essence of your being. You aren't defined by their opinions of you. Always be transparent, accountable, and honest; but don't compensate for those who are afraid to love you.

Love is only scary
when you accept the disguises.
Love is only scary
when you worship the idea of it.

Giving someone the privilege of my forgiveness when they don't deserve it would only deepen my wound. The irony, I will heal regardless. The closure is the broken pieces of me. The lessons shaped me. I forgive myself and I will do it without feeling like a hostage. I will do it without feeling like a burden.

If you forever run
from the demons that haunt you,
you will always accept the love
that hurts you.

PICK ME

Nothing brings the heart more turmoil than the need to be chosen. The yearning to be desired. The *thrill* of that fleeting moment and the constant chase to feel it again.

Unrequited love is the fantasy you envisioned and prayed for, but never got to touch. The love that always slipped through your fingers. The love that never was enough, even at the capacity of giving yourself away.

My moment of truth was when I realized my heart couldn't be broken because of the lack of love I received. It could only be broken by giving it to the mercy of those who didn't want it.

Don't settle for a love that's disguised as pain, a never-ending battle of heartache. Don't accept every offer that comes your way; not everyone will bring the best version of you out. Find it within you first so you won't accept any version of someone.

Timing is everything, but it won't make
something not for you, right for you.
Timing will only bring you two things:
a lesson and a blessing. It's rare for both to be
a part of the same story.

NOVEMBER 20, 2020
6:09 PM

If I loved you, I loved you, maybe not enough to bare my soul to you. You may have brought comfort but not protection; you didn't make me feel free, you caged me in. Many didn't understand my free spirit, so they let me go. Many didn't understand my growth, because of the constant tries to discredit it and trying their best to stunt it. *I loved them very much, they opened my heart and taught me how to love, how to care for another soul, and how to give. They also taught me what love isn't, what heartbreak feels like, and what boundaries are.*

They taught me what love feels like but not what's like to be loved.
They taught me how to give but never receive. They taught me the more you show your authentic soul, the more you'll lose but the more you gain... because with an intense heart like mine, the energy alone tells you everything. I wasn't afraid to find the souls who love me in my vulnerability, completely naked, baring my soul, I knew someone would feel me.

Once upon a time I was naïve, I believed
there was something worth fighting for in
someone who brought me heartache
because I loved them and I thought love
would cure my sickness; until I was left to
grieve the loss of someone I thought of as
my end game. We don't know where it
starts and where it ends; we just hope to
have this feeling for as long as it lasts. I
don't believe the right person comes at the
wrong time because I would have treated
them with grace; I would have loved them
tenderly, without hesitation. I wouldn't
have to be without their love. I wouldn't be
grieving a loss I could have saved myself
from. I don't believe the right person would
ever destroy me because of bad timing; they
wouldn't destroy me at all.

FLIP THE SCRIPT, LOOK WITHIN

We can love someone and still bring them pain because sometimes it's not about them at all; it's about us and what we're running from. Even when our intentions are good doesn't mean they're aligned. We do things out of love that only lead to disappointment. We abandon someone because we know what they want isn't something we can give, but we allowed them to believe we could because the feeling was too good. We just want to feel something. We hurt people because we're afraid to face our brokenness instead; we let them in to take their best shot and we lose. We can love someone but fear hurting them because we don't trust our hearts; we know it will only end in disappointment, so we constantly cause destruction. It has nothing to do with being a coward or a terrible human; sometimes we're just lost souls looking to be understood; we accept love and ruin it without intending. *Sometimes we're so afraid of feeling something real because we fear not being deserving of it.*

We don't always deserve what we go
through, but it doesn't change what's done.
You have the power to change the outcome.
You survived.
You're more resilient because of it.
Your trauma is only a reflection of you,
it doesn't define you.

JANUARY 3, 2023
12:05 PM

Nothing in life is *easy*. When people say **"easier said than done"** it makes me wonder what they believe other people have been through; because everything I worked for wasn't easy and I did it because I deserved to be happy and not soak in the same storyline my whole life. Saying "it's not easy" is like pushing it to the side because you have no faith in a good outcome. You possess the power; it's all in your mind. To be better, you need to become better. You need to believe you deserve better; to attract better. Nothing in life will just be handed to you. It's never easy, but it's worth it.

I don't wait until the new year to *purge* the outgrown and unwarranted. I part my ways when it's presented; I don't overstay my welcome. I don't need 365 days to do a cleanse. My energy is too sacred to keep draining myself for people and things that have outlived their time in my life; breaking the pattern is immediate because I refuse to fall into the unhealthy cycle of the past version of me.

LOST FLIES

I'm not selfish, I let people breathe and have
the space to clear their minds; but there's a
difference between a bad day and
completely shutting someone out, taking
everything out on them when it has nothing
to do with them. In a connection,
communication is everything. How do I
know to respect your silence if you don't
tell me you need time? How do I know
everything will be okay if all you do is act
as if nothing happened? Silence can kill a lot
of things, especially when communication
stays absent.

A REMINDER

Telling someone *"don't let it bother you"* is equivalent to telling someone to suppress their feelings and be emotionless. Allow them to express how they feel. Guiding yourself through the emotion helps you understand what triggers you; it also helps you never allow the same energy in your orbit again.

I wasn't interested in being accepted, especially when it came to a crowd I didn't fit into. I never forced a connection with people who never felt me. I might have misunderstood my purpose; I might have chased for love, but I never made someone feel like I needed them. I never thought someone could fill me with the courage to love myself with every part of myself I took for granted.

I wasn't interested in being someone's doormat, but that didn't mean I never let people stay longer than their time granted. I can't lie and say I didn't try and make things work when they were overdue to be outgrown. I can't say I never let someone walk all over me and made me believe their love was something I needed.

I wasn't interested in making connections that lead me nowhere. I wasn't interested in putting my heart into something that wouldn't give me a story. I wasn't interested in wasting a moment trying to be understood by someone who couldn't comprehend. I wasn't interested in being told my worth by people who couldn't love themselves.

HOPELESS SOUL

I couldn't tell you why I chose to let people come and go when it was time to be real. I couldn't tell you why I tried to keep people around who weren't a permanent stay. I couldn't tell you why I thought loving myself wasn't as important when it came to allowing someone else to touch my heart. I never understood how my love for them could be honest if I couldn't even be real with myself. I felt like a coward *trying to provide a love I couldn't give myself.*

Accept sometimes people disappear from your life only for a blessing to appear. The universe will never take something away from you without giving you something much more beautiful.

Let go of what's gone.

Never let your heart turn cold, you owe it to yourself to keep loving. Being cold will only bring you pain; find warmth in your heart. Your love deserves to be felt. You have too much heart to be cold; just because you live in a world that's afraid to show their heart.

Healing is something you will always practice. Growing is constant. You don't need to be fully healed to love and be loved, but you need to be healed in a way you don't forget to break that cycle or set that boundary. Healing is learning what you once accepted isn't what you deserve. Healing is creating a healthier you.

GHOSTING

People hear the word ghosting and assume you're a coward, you're toxic, and you lack accountability if you choose that road—they will call it abuse. I feel we don't talk enough about the other side of ghosting, the one where silence saves you. People hear the word ghosting and assume you walked away without speaking a word, that an explanation is always deserved. What about the situation where you're constantly shut out and desperately looking to be heard, but they're not there to listen? What about the situation when you spoke your truths, and your concerns and all you receive are "I'm sorry" and a continued pattern of the same old story? What about the situation where you're abused and there's no other way? What about when you said all you could and did everything you could, to save what you thought you had but you're the only one fighting to keep it together? Is ghosting the wrong choice when you've become a prisoner in your mind? Is ghosting the wrong choice when you leave to save yourself? Someone who doesn't care if they destroy you — won't care if you choose your sanity. I don't care how anyone tries to justify it; not everyone deserves an explanation of why they hurt you. Not everyone deserves a third chance. Not everyone deserves your heart in their hands, to keep playing you, using you, while you're trying to find the words to express, to escape them. You don't need to apologize for doing what's best for you, especially to those who only poisoned you.

Sometimes people don't know what they want, so they will take you along for the ride until they decide. They will tell beautiful lies and twisted fantasies. They will use your weakness, those three words to claim you. The manipulative language they set in their ways. You let your guard down when they reassure you they are here to stay. The way they play with your heart but you think maybe this time will be different, but you end up at the same ending to the same story. You will only be deserving of what you settle for, it's the heartbreaking truth. The more you allow, the more they continue. You need to be strong enough to know the love you feel for them may never come full circle and it is okay to part ways. You will find love, real love, and it won't feel like this.

It is *incredibly dangerous to fall in love with the fantasy of someone*, to create this ideal love you're searching for without a boundary in the site. They want to be loved unconditionally but have no idea you are settling for the conditions of what they are giving, without the conditions you should be placed to not find yourself broken. We all start somewhere. We all have been starved of time, affection, and attention. We all craved a love we never touched. A love that we never even gave ourselves. Why is it that we look elsewhere and never within? It is because we feel someone else can love the parts of us we are so uncomfortable with, maybe they can teach us how to love what is within. The cycle continues to disrupt your journey when you allow someone in, to try and pick up the pieces you left broken — because mending them yourself seems lonely. We cannot expect someone to heal us, we can not even expect them to help us. It is our responsibility to love our brokenness so we can find someone to be ours without setting a solid foundation on our own. We cannot expect someone to read our minds, to know what we need, to know what we are struggling to find within. It is a dangerous journey, *searching for love in all the wrong places and all the wrong hearts*. We deserve a love that opens our hearts intending to hold us in a way that will not destroy everything we built inside. We deserve love, a healthy love, one that doesn't make us question our worth.

It is so frightening to wear your heart on your sleeve, to always follow your heart.
It's the scariest thing in the world,
to give your most intimate parts to someone
when there is no guarantee
you won't lose that love.

Sometimes you need to stop
watering dead plants
and start creating an environment
for new ones to grow within.

I Was Never Broken: Volume 3

I broke my heart every time I acted like I
wasn't hurt just to spare someone else pain.

I broke my heart when I allowed myself to
turn cold when I knew I couldn't survive it.

I broke my heart when I locked away my love
and broke my soul. I craved connection.
I craved to feel. It was dangerous to try and
tame an empath like me, *vulnerability was
my superpower*.

I used to be the sad soul — I used it as my excuse to blame love for the countless mistakes I made. I accepted love from some that were not whole. I accepted love from some who chose to love me when it was convenient. I accepted love from some who chose to love me in private and showcase me as the bad guy to the world. I accepted all forms of love. I chose to stay around to fix some. I chose to try and move forward and give second chances that weren't deserved. I chose to forgive instead of holding grudges. I chose to settle. I chose to stay where I felt familiar because starting over was terrifying. Comfort felt good. I chose to hold on when it was best for me to go. Love was never a choice for me. I loved everyone even if they hurt me. I loved when it wasn't reciprocated. I loved when I let go. I couldn't help but show my heart, I just wish I spent more time making it healthy.

SELF-LOVE

It's a beautiful thing —
to love who you are
and not give that love up.

It's a beautiful thing —
to give yourself the same effort
you pour into everyone else.

Those who take advantage know they can take without having to give, are ones who are not worthy of any piece of your heart that you have to give. Anyone who leaves should not get another chance to rekindle your love because your passion was too intense for them in the first place.

Some people don't deserve second chances.

I wish I could take it back when I pretended like someone didn't hurt me. I let it snowball into the trauma that was passed down to everyone who loved me. I convinced myself the feeling was too intense because it turned some off. I don't know why I allowed someone to treat my vulnerability as a weakness until I became emotionally closed off.

HOPELESS VISION

I tend to see the good in everyone.
I tend to try to keep alive
the good I saw in them.
I never wanted to believe love was
unhappiness, desolation, and a pest.
I refused to believe
love was a mess
Imperfect maybe, but never destruction.
I believed the broken deserve a home too.

I never thought
I lost nothing when we parted,
letting you go was my *greatest* blessing.

Nurture your heart and heal the parts of you before you let someone close. Meet your demons, it's not fair to anyone to fall in love with a work in progress when they deserve someone ready to embrace them. Someone who won't hurt them. *You deserve that too.*

JANUARY 7, 2022
11:19 PM

I searched for happiness in everyone that came with a spark. I created gardens within connections that had no growth. I continued to go back and take back those who didn't make me feel safe but brought comfort because of the habit—the codependency formed by being with them. I chased the temporary highs, none of which brought me peace. I had to sit with the ugly, the truth—I was allowing people to come in without proper boundaries. I was allowing people to fill a space in my heart, even my soul the one place that I locked away, to keep reserved for those who deserved me. I lost balance way along the way. I couldn't decipher what was real anymore. I had to be uncomfortable. I had to see myself as not only the victim but the one allowed to be taken advantage of. I played a part in my agony. There was always going to be someone who wronged me, but when I finally took accountability for my mistakes, the story stopped replaying everything I was giving was coming back to me.

FEBRUARY 25, 2022
12:54 AM

Being with you, I don't think you realize how much I stop in thought and it passes my mind, how I couldn't be happier. How being with you makes me feel beautiful. It makes up for the lost love and the times I was fighting hard to be loved. It makes every phase before feel like a lesson, one to prepare me for being with you. You are so special, so divine. You are one of a kind. The way you pull my heartstrings. The way you bring a smile on my darkest days. How you effortlessly bring joy and bliss after endless days wondering if I would ever find someone like you, being emotionally closed off for years with a wall up, I wasn't afraid to embrace you. I met you and knew it was you and would always be you. Not many people are fortunate enough to find love like this. I promise, with every vessel. I will cherish, nourish, and always allow our love to grow.

NOTE TO SELF:

Don't make excuses for people who hurt you.
The story played out how it did, even if it
was something deeper within them, you
didn't deserve to be dragged through hell.
You shouldn't be punished because you
loved someone who couldn't appreciate
themselves.

We need to start *celebrating*
happiness around us more.
We need to start putting
more *love* into the world,
to receive the same **blessings** in return.

I trusted my heart more than my intuition when it came to letting someone in. I longed to be loved, I didn't have certain expectations which is why I got robbed of every beautiful fantasy I envisioned. I was shadowed by doubt but the aspiration to be loved was the core of my madness. The deception, darkness, and relentless fight to prove my love. I wish I fought to be more respected than accepted. I wish I could have saved some love for myself. I wish I saved the effort but without the loss, I wouldn't have discovered *my heart is treasure*.

JANUARY 4, 2022
2:37 PM

It was not until I took accountability for my wrongs and the pain I inflicted onto others, the universe guided me to what was meant for me. Everything started aligning when I wasn't afraid to face the consequences of my actions and when I was no longer hiding from my truth. I brought a lot of pain to others when I blamed only them when I wasn't fully aware of my wrongs. I brought a lot of pain myself when I was blinded by the damage I brought to every connection when I didn't heal myself first. It was a story I replayed often, being wronged by others, feeling worthless, and not being good enough. It was a story that I kept accepting because it was all I knew. I took accountability for doing others wrong in the crossfire. I took accountability for allowing them to take advantage of me often. Everything I deserved, everything I desired, aligned with me once I allowed the truth to flow in.

I look at you and I see myself,
I look at myself and see you.
When I look at us, it's a **broken** view.

written by my sixteen-year-old self

It's crazy how it can only take days, maybe minutes to love someone, but it takes years to forget someone. To some, it might take years to build that love and only seconds to break it.

written by my sixteen-year-old self

DECEMBER 6, 2016
2:00 PM

I learned not every situation you come by needs a reaction, and that sometimes things should be left how they ended but to always make sure you're happy with how it ended. You don't want to live the rest of your life wondering if you should have done something different. I never saw it coming, but I saw it go. People change, things change, and we need to learn to let go and remember how things used to be. I'm blessed to be alive. I'm blessed to have wonderful people in my corner. I'm blessed to have the opportunities and things I already accomplished. I have no hate in my heart for people that were once a part of my life because I once loved them and probably will always but it doesn't matter because when you're not seen for who you are and just the image, they made of you it's gone. For the ones who are patient with me when I'm distant, thank you. I'm trying to figure myself out and where I'm going in life. Time to let go of everything that once was and be happy with everything I have.

Why be a copy,
when you're the writer of your own life?

written by my sixteen-year-old self

I never met anyone who lived a *fairytale* and hasn't been loved, left, or traumatized. There's a difference between love meant for you and love you accept. There's a difference between love from settling and love with foundation and boundaries. Nothing in life is a fairytale, but in my story, the love meant for me came at the most unexpected time, after the pain and heartbreak, after I picked up the pieces and found, embraced, and loved myself.

The *purest* souls get hurt the most.
The saddest part of all,
they turn into someone they don't
recognize.

I'm a *lover and a healer*,
I care too much about making sure
everyone is comfortable, loved, and
understood. I let the emotions of everyone
impact me. I need to learn not to let their
projections ruin me. I need to learn I can
love them without trying to fix them.

People that made me feel *uncomfortable* in
my transitional period have no access to my
growth. You didn't believe in me. You
didn't see the vision.

Healing is so painful yet so breathtaking,
watching your broken pieces drift into the
memory of everything you once loved and
meeting the version of you that you honor.

CONFESSIONS

My life was a sad song on repeat. I lacked passion. I
lacked ambition. The only thing that kept me
going was the idea of love I had envisioned.
Countless times I was let down and left broken.
I was empty waiting for someone to pour their
love, inspiration, and bliss into me. Self-love was
a puzzle I left unfinished because chasing the
love from others gave me temporary comfort. I
was addicted to feeling wanted and that
moment of weakness of lust kept me going.
Maybe I was used to being used and left alone.
Maybe loneliness was all my story told. I was
completely beside myself, the vision I had
planned no longer existed because when
someone who felt good came along I ghosted
before it could be something real. I was afraid of
the fantasy. I was afraid I could be loved the
way I always wanted to be, but this time around
I didn't think I was deserving enough to be.
What if I hurt them? What if I couldn't be
enough?

♥

MOONCHILD

This crisp 50-degree winter afternoon. It's a new year and I'm sitting here watching the water glide down the lake, wondering where it goes and where it ends. How something so simple can be so breathtaking. I sit here and I aspire to be as peaceful as the way the sun hits the water as it starts to set and give the moon its time to shine. I feel complete when I'm surrounded by nature. It's one of the moments I feel inspired. It captives me and welcomes me home. I feel aligned. I feel connected. I always find myself back in this same place whenever I need a reset. It's like I can look out and feel my energy flowing — my whole mind, heart, and soul are fulfilled. A beautiful view. *A beautiful place to call my sanctuary.*

I watched you *break*
I watched you mend
I watched you battle
I watched you lose
I watched you *learn*
I watched you bruise
I watched you regret
I watched you repent
I watched you hurt
I watched you **love**
I watched you give
I watched you overcome
I watched you heal
I watched you **bloom**

LETTERS FROM MY INNER CHILD

I watched you shed the old layers. I listened when you cried your heart out. I was there when you shut down and shut everyone out. I was the inner voice keeping you dreaming. I was the inner feeling keeping you believing. When you felt your lowest, did you feel me hug you tight? When you would overthink, did you hear me talk you down? It was uncomfortable for me to watch you break, recreate, and grow but I was there holding your hand and pouring into you when you didn't have the strength to keep going because you were learning.

Goodbyes can cure you —
forgiveness is optional.
Both paths don't need to be aligned,

The healing process
is like an overdue apology,
don't be afraid to collect —
to cleanse.

- *remedies for the soul*

JANUARY 1, 2023
3:04 PM

I never wanted to be remembered as the one who got away because all I ever did was fight to stay. I always gave my all even when it wasn't deserved, even when I lost my worth. I never knew if it was right to stay under the conditions of keeping what we had alive but my intentions were aligned. I didn't want to walk away and wonder "what if "and resent us. *I only wanted to be remembered for my pure heart.*

I don't wish the worst on anyone if they hurt
me. I don't want to live with that kind of
karma. You see, I believe people can
change. I believe everyone can grow, but
that's if they choose to bloom into what
they're afraid of. I believe everyone hides a
layer of themselves they're afraid to face —
insecurities take control of one's ego and
pride gets in the way. I believe there are
many layers of people and the ones who
hurt the most are the ones who hurt within.
I know we all can hurt people because once
you are hurt, you become a wrecking ball
until you find your way through and out of
your way. Everyone I loved didn't always
return that love because no one I loved was
obligated to reciprocate a love that wasn't
honest, and it was on me when I made it
harder than it had to be. I learned some
connections were meant to break. I learned
some people were meant to hurt me, shape
me, and help me build this relationship
with myself that I lacked all these years. A
healthy love with myself, I should have
started there.

♥

Sometimes we *over-love*
when it's time to outgrow.

I survived every storm
that came my way —
the struggle to stay afloat,
as the tide turned
I made my way.
I turned something messy,
disastrous and cold
into serenity, tranquility, and warmth.

- *the aftermath*

The *grass isn't always greener*
on the other side,
doesn't mean you need to stay
on the side,
the grass doesn't grow.

We all were born to stand out.
We all were made to be beautiful.
It just takes years to acknowledge
we don't need to fit in,
our beauty comes from within.

Sometimes your expectations
can ruin how beautiful something truly is.
Sometimes the beauty is right there
but you can't embrace it
because you're always expecting more.

TAKE YOUR BEST SHOT

Handle me with care. Be gentle with my heart.
Don't make this another heartbreak
on my list of regrets. I won't come for
revenge but karma will pay your dues. It
will humble you. Please, know the risks
before taking my heart for a ride you can't
see through. *Don't love me if you don't plan to
love your hardest.*

Don't forget how much courage it takes to love yourself after years of loathing who you'd become. Don't forget how brave it is to always show up, to love your hardest, and always pick yourself back up after every letdown. Don't forget how much strength it takes to not fall back into old schemes of envy and not feeling good enough. Don't forget it takes patience, time, and effort to see the growth—to feel the healing. Don't forget to see the beauty, even in your darkest moments.

DEAR MOON

You are captivating, I admire the way you shine in your darkest hour. I aspire to bring the same comfort you inspire. I find myself searching for you, but without much effort, you're there looking down on me. I feel aligned and empowered with you by my side. I allow my emotions to flow and no longer hide. The way you drain old energy and provide a spiritual cleanse. I vow to always love myself the way you always show up and remind me. I aspire to one day be as beautiful as you.

Celebrating myself more. Giving myself the flowers I deserve, I'm not waiting for anyone to show up and make me deserving of them. I nurture my own. I heal my soul. I know I'm worthy enough. I won't wait for anyone to validate me.

More love.
More *inspiration*.
More *comfort* spaces for more souls
to come and feel at home.

I was once someone who wanted to be loved at any cost, even when it meant giving up myself. I had low standards for love when I let anyone occupy my heart because they made me feel special. They spoke all the words I wanted to hear; they did everything to prove I should let them in until the chase for love no longer existed and I'm face to face with this person and I no longer have the passion that I had when I was fighting for them. I think it's when I realized they didn't bring me the spark I desperately needed or the space to grow as an individual. When they showed up, they brought themselves to the table but didn't bring inspiration, support, or growth. They didn't believe they needed to bring anything more than themselves; because it was the love I was looking for, and they were right; but as I grew I learned it wasn't just about love, it was about someone who challenged me in a way that showed me there is more that exists within. That's when I realized I'd rather be with someone who shows me there's more to me than just being loved.

Every time I got let down I always blamed my heart. I began to feel like my happiness was the enemy. I began to feel like love wasn't for me. I blamed my heart because of the times I would overuse it. I blamed my heart for all the times I abused it. I blamed my heart for the countless times I chose to give more knowing it would crush me. I realized my heart could do no wrong because even after I've done wrong, my heart still craved more. My heart was never to blame, instead, I was for all the times I overworked it.

"Only expose me to good"
"Only expose me to real"
"Only expose me to honest"

…except it's impossible.
The darkness is a stepping stone to the
goodness you seek. The darkness is the
realness of the story you're trying to be
freed from. The darkness is honesty, just
with sorrow, until you learn to detach from
the thought of nothing good can come from
the dark moments—how else would it be
possible to find the light?

Unlearning things from my past was a challenge I thought I'd never overcome.

Unlearning to unlove because I was the only one who loved, what I received back was the bare minimum of what I settled for love to be.

Unlearning patterns because falling for anyone who made me feel something had me mistaken for something real.

Unlearning comfort in the form of codependency had made me believe they were for me and no one else could be.

OBLIGATED LOVE

I'm responsible for how I choose to show up in this world. I'm accountable for the decisions I choose to make. I'm the one who sits with my thoughts and creates a safe place for them to live without wandering to the dark side. I'm the one who takes care of my being because I know exactly what I need. I'm taking care of myself mentally, emotionally, and physically. I know many love me and show up for me but learning to love myself has saved me. My only obligation is to myself.

♥

BUTTERFLY EFFECT

I am slowly finding my way back to myself. I have moments where I allow myself to be consumed by my thoughts because they may be around to teach me something. I am slowly finding my way through. I have moments where I loathe myself and fall into the same cycle of wondering what's my purpose, what's my balance, and what comes next. I am slowly finding love within and it's a constant battle to fight the urge to allow my insecurities to mold me. I am slowly finding my way to wholeness. I have moments of doubt and moments I overthink until it becomes overkill, but I am slowly finding my balance. I am learning patience when it comes to discovering who I am because there's always a layer of me I haven't met. *I am slowly finding my way* to understanding I'll forever be a work in process, but one that transcends beautifully without stunting my growth. I am slowly embracing the beauty of the butterfly I was purposely created to be.

♥

THE GRAY AREA

The gray area with no hues of the blues, it's more like you're numb to the world around you. There's no purpose in sight and you're lost with no direction to fight. You feel depleted and there's no replenishing, you don't stand the chance to keep going. You feel stagnant and everything around you keeps circling trying to open your eyes, but you keep yourself closed off to every opportunity that could cure you. You stand in this place of chaos because it's the only time you feel something remotely real, but you don't realize you're digging yourself deeper into this unhealed place. The gray area with only clouds in site, even on the most beautiful days seems melancholy. The gray area is the era of our transitional period. It's the moment of utter paralysis, it's the wake-up call.

♥

FARWELL

The hardest goodbye is the one you didn't see coming, that's why I always feared the unknown because of the torture it brings.

The hardest goodbye is the one where you don't get to declare until they're no longer breathing. The one where you're face to face with their lifelessness and you don't have the words to express it because this kind of grief wasn't expected.

The hardest goodbye is the one where you don't hold the capacity to change the outcome, so you pack up old love, feelings, and memories and gift them with the freedom to no longer hold you, hostage. **The goodbye that was long overdue**.

The hardest goodbye is the one where you peacefully allow yourself to transcend to the next chapter of your journey. The goodbye to the old pieces and versions of you.

♥

HEARTBREAK RECEIPT

In every heartbreak, I always walked away with myself and a lesson, one I needed to go through to see the silver lining. I learned a lot about myself in ways of what I would accept and what I refuse to allow to consume me over again. I learned not every heartbreak was intentional, some were not for me so they couldn't be what I needed them to be. I learned not everyone who cared for me was love-stuck and their infatuation never made it full circle to an everlasting bond. I learned the pain isn't always personal, sometimes others' projections and reflections caused their wounds to bleed onto me, and I was there to try my hardest to mend them. I learned a trauma bond wouldn't ever be more than a business deal. I learned I couldn't ever love someone enough to love me back. *In every heartbreak,* I learned I was always going to be worthy of whatever I was accepting. I needed to be better, always, to attract better. *Heartbreak* liberated me. *Heartbreak* brought me the clarity to see everyone deserves to walk away from pain with healthier intentions and a healed soul.

♥

I feel like there will always be certain
people in our lives we always end up giving
more effort than we receive in return. It's
just for you to decide what boundaries to
set and whether it's a connection you think
will outlive the darkest times.

FORGIVE AND FORGET

The term *"forgive and forget"* is so misleading because you truly never forget unless you spend years suppressing your memories. Forgiving is giving yourself the space to heal even if the person isn't worthy of your forgiveness at the moment. Forgiveness is giving yourself permission to move on without feeling like a hostage. Forgiving is like your first breath after coming up from drowning. It takes time and patience to be in a place to forgive someone. It takes time to understand everything that happened to you. It takes time for you to forgive yourself for allowing it. Forgetting is something that doesn't escape you as much as you wish it away, you will always remember. You will always have that lesson to look back on and reflect on, to remember what to never do or allow ever again. Find your peace there.

I have only desired connections that inspired me, not ones that depleted me. I have only desired bonds that fueled me, never ones that took every piece of me without any chance of repair. I have only desired connections that brought life to me, never ones that left me lifeless.

SELF-LOVE

Self-love begins as soon as you choose yourself. It starts when you leave behind the life you wanted that wasn't yours and embrace the life that's awaiting you.

Self-love isn't hard but we treat it like it's a battlefield because we are constantly fighting the demons that keep us from loving what's within.

Self-love begins once you stop doubting yourself, your potential, and what you bring to the table. You will only feel further away from yourself worrying about those who can't accept your presence.

Self-love is validating yourself in the absence of everyone who couldn't appreciate you.

Self-love begins once you take control of your power and embody every layer of who you are, the layers you shed, and the versions you've yet to meet.

Self-love is your greatest love story.

♥

A LETTER TO MY THIRTIES

We're starting a new era of us. I'm ready for
what's to come. I'm ready for the lessons and
the continued blessings to shower me and teach
me more about what's underneath these layers
of me I've yet to know. I'm ready to embrace the
parts of me that will follow me forever; the parts
I need to love harder than others. I'm ready to
face what's to come, even though I have faith it's
going to be better. I'm ready to face my
weaknesses as they appear and to become more
resilient as I grow. I'm ready to live my best and
to continue to keep the ones around me that
only help me strive to be a better version of
myself. I'm ready to inspire, love, and give
myself to those who are willing to feel me, hear
me, and love me. I'm ready to keep pouring and
watering this version of myself that continues to
bloom, and that continues to make me proud.
I'm ready for the **best chapter of my life**.

♥

OCTOBER 12, 2022
12:28 PM

I don't expect everyone to relate to my story.
Putting my work out there was never about
it being agreed with, it was because I loved
writing and I wanted to free myself from
not having a voice. This is my voice. I don't
expect everyone to understand my story
because we all have unique ones. For those
who find themselves in my work — it's
something truly special knowing we both
have been at a place where we felt
something similar but still very different.
The most comforting thing of all is to know
we're never alone. When it comes to my
books, my story, my healing. I'm expressing
myself the best way I know how. I'm
blessed to be a source of peace for those
who need to hear the same words I write.
I'm blessed to have a platform that allows
me to be vulnerable and express my true
self in the rawest form. So please, be kind

and understand I'm not a therapist. I don't
have the answers. I don't give advice.

The only thing I could give you is inspiration, to
always follow your heart and never let
anyone tell you that you're wrong about
how you feel. Don't hide who you are from
anyone. Don't dim yourself to be loved.
Don't change who you are to be accepted.
Love yourself the same way you give love
to everyone. The most important thing, live
while you have the chance. Don't have any
regrets — only lessons learned. You'll look at
life so much differently and your heart
won't feel as heavy when it comes to
moving on. You're resilient, always
remember that.

I Was Never Broken: Volume 3

Thank you for taking the time to read my story, I know no one is obligated to buy my books which makes it even more of a blessing to have people out there **supporting** me and giving my voice a purpose. Thank you for supporting my dream. Thank you for giving my work life. Writing is my therapy and I'm so happy to share my therapy and know that it has touched, healed, and inspired a lot of people.

I Was Never Broken: Volume 3

SOCIAL MEDIA PLATFORMS:

Facebook: Moonsoulchild
Twitter: Bymoonsoulchild
Tiktok: Bymoonsoulchild
Instagram: Moonsoulchild
Apple Music: Moonsoulchild
Spotify: Moonsoulchild

Moonsoulchild.com

THIS SERIES INCLUDES:

I Was Never Broken **Volume 1**
I Was Never Broken *Volume 2*

Cover art by myself